BLOKES & SHEDS

BLOKES&SHEDS

MARK THOMSON

Angus&Robertson
An imprint of HarperCollins*Publishers*

Angus&Robertson
An imprint of HarperCollins*Publishers,* Australia

First published in Australia in 1995
by HarperCollins*Publishers* Pty Limited
ACN 009 913 517
A member of the HarperCollins*Publishers* (Australia) Pty Limited Group
Reprinted in 1995, 1996 (six times), 1997

HarperCollins*Publishers*
25 Ryde Road, Pymble, Sydney, NSW 2073, Australia
31 View Road, Glenfield, Auckland 10, New Zealand
77-85 Fulham Palace Road, London W6 8JB, United Kingdom
Hazelton Lanes, 55 Avenue Road, Suite 2900, Toronto, Ontario M5R 3L2
and 1995 Markham Road, Scarborough, Ontario M1B 5M8, Canada
10 East 53rd Street, New York NY 10032, USA

National Library of Australia Cataloguing-in-Publication data:

Thomson, Mark, 1955 –   .
Blokes & sheds.
ISBN 0 207 18916 1.
1. Outhouses – Social aspects – Australia.
2. Toolshed Social aspects – Australia. I. Title.
392.36

Photography by Mark Thomson
Printed in Australia by McPherson's Printing Group

12 11 10 9   97 98 99

Contents

Acknowledgments

For their assistance and inspiration, my thanks to: Dave Glazbrook, Leon Earle, Eric Algra, Jennifer Layther, Annabelle Collett, Tony and Terry from Yodel Action, Helen Fuller, Michael Lee, Dave Whyte, John Schumann, Les Lloyd, Francesco Barbaro, Tubby Justice and, especially, to my daughter, Billie, who enjoys hammering nails into timber offcuts.

My special thanks to the hundreds of shed owners who allowed me inside their sheds and shared their thoughts with me.

All photographs were shot with an Olympus OM2 using a 28 mm lens on Ilford FP4 rated at 125 ASA, using existing light. My thanks to Deborah Workman for her care and commitment in the darkroom.

"You can do anything in a shed" — Gary

Now there's a good shed . . .

Sheds are an integral part of Australian life. No other nation values them as we do. Despite this, our sheds, modest from the outside yet glorious on the inside, have never really been recorded or their many purposes explained. Sheds come and go with no-one the wiser, remaining secret and mysterious places that are exposed only at a garage sale or on the death of their owners. The purpose of this book is to throw some light on why the backyard shed sustains life and meaning for so many men.

In a shed the rules are different. Here, chaos is allowed to reign, asserting its creative force in wayward contrast to the suburban order all around. It's a place that permits the presence of spiders, sawdust and stinks. The acrid smell of gardening chemicals mixes with the reek of damp, mould and old oil; light softened through dusty windows never gets to the murky corners. Danger lurks. Hidden in rough painted cupboards are forbidden chemicals. Rusting nails lie scattered around the floor, ready to pierce unprotected feet. Screeching power tools send sparks flying. Risks and thrills are everywhere.

Old biscuit tins and Vegemite jars full of nails, screws and washers await the pleasure of being sorted and reused. Tobacco tins bursting with bits of wire, broken plugs, old glasses and pieces of machined steel — clearly a part of some device only to be wondered at — squat on sagging shelves. Never throw them out. Their time will come.

A shed can be a reservoir of memories and experience, rich with satisfying layers of accumulated personal history.

Time can stand still here, making it a place for meditation and contemplation. Some men go to their sheds to escape from family responsibilities, never really to emerge again. Others make their sheds the centre of family and community life, using them as places for preparing food, brewing beer, making music, playing sports, sharing information and generally socialising.

Sheds transcend class. All sorts of people, rich and poor, city and country, are sustained by their sheds. Anyone with the modest luxury of a reasonably sized building block can construct one in their backyard.

Sheds also transcend age. Young men go to them to be initiated into the mysterious art of making a motor vehicle go or brewing beer, while retired men take advantage of the quietude to work and yet not work — an opportunity to tinker away their twilight years.

Our national knack for invention and innovation, for making do, lives on in the shed. The "she'll be right" attitude may be denigrated as the blight of Australian industry, but it thrives in the country's backyards. And it's this do-it-yourself ethos that gives the shed supremacy. A shed is a palace of practicality where a bloke is the ruler.

In this book you'll find just some of the types of sheds that grace our backyards. Like their contents, sheds come in all shapes and sizes and their purposes range the spectrum. What binds them is something undefinable, something as mysterious as the dark corners of their interiors — something that happens when a bloke gets a shed.

Definitions

In Australia a shed can be anything from a dunny-size construction to an aircraft hangar covering an acre or two. A shed might be defined as a building outside or away from the main domestic living space. However, this doesn't go far enough; a rumpus room can demonstrate shed-like qualities, even though it's part of the house. Perhaps what really makes a shed a shed is the value placed on it by its owner.

A garage is not a shed: it's simply a place in which to store a car. However a garage can, given a little care and attention, become a shed. Many of the sheds included here could also be called home workshops.

Shed, *n. a rough structure or lean-to, built for shelter, storage etc. (Medieval English* shadde, *Old English* scead, sced *shelter, shade)*

In choosing sheds to include in this book, an important criterion for selection was that their owners or occupiers were men. That's not to say that women don't have sheds or other special spaces, but the link between men and sheds is a strong one. Australian blokes like their sheds and spend a lot of time in them.

Sheds are not uniquely Australian. Many countries have similar domestic spaces: America has its basements, for instance. However, in Australia the average home has plenty of space, and our standard of living is high enough to allow for the cost of spare domestic buildings.

The basic model

This hay shed, perched like a strange giant insect high on a windy hill,
says it all: a roof to keep the rain off and provide some shade.
Getting out of the weather is a good start.

Rural origins

In many a discussion about sheds you'll hear blokes talk about what a great one their grandfather, uncle or father had on the farm.

The ability to fix anything with a few basic materials and a streak of ingenuity is firmly entrenched in Australian folklore. There has been a deeply ingrained suspicion that store-bought gear, with its flashy packaging, is ultimately mere trickery, and that there's always a tool, method or shortcut that can do the job.

The grand tradition of do-it-yourself goes back to the beginning of white settlement. With transport slow and distances from cities great, an ability to solve any number of small engineering or manufacturing problems was necessary for a farmer's survival. A broken plough could not be repaired by a quick phone call or a part trucked up from the city overnight. The problem had to be fixed through ingenuity and resourcefulness.

This aptitude for nifty solutions with a length of fencing wire, a hammer and a piece of 4" x 2" timber is strongly ingrained and widely felt to be some sort of national competitive advantage. People take pride in such skills, even when more sensible solutions may be available.

While we like to evoke this tradition of backyard self-sufficiency, most people now live in the capital cities, and the majority of Australian men wouldn't know how to fix a Southern Cross windmill or tell the difference between wheat and barley. The ideal of the self-sufficient handyman nevertheless persists, manifested in the domestic shed.

Meanwhile farmers, always practical and level-headed, don't stand for this kind of sentimental mush. As farm machinery has grown a lot larger and mechanically more sophisticated, the average farm shed is now more likely to resemble a small factory or a truck-repair workshop. Heavy vehicles such as semi-trailers are now common on farms. The romantic stone or timber shed is almost a thing of the past. The practical farm shed is now more likely to be the size of a small aeroplane hangar. It's not easy to get the same character into a vast echoing steel cube.

The Stumpenschuppen

John likes old country buildings. So much so that he dismantled this one made of interlocked mallee roots and painstakingly reassembled it on his own property some distance away.

When he was finished, John invited some locals from the nearby pub to admire his handiwork. They got out of the car — and promptly fell about laughing. "You've made the walls too straight," they said.

Stumpenschuppen have surprisingly effective insulation properties, especially when the inside wall is given a coating of mud. Early farmers often built and lived in them on arrival to this country, as they could be built almost entirely from found natural materials.

Ron's implement shed

Ron and his wife Glenda live out in the Mallee on a 800-acre farm first settled
by Ron's father before the First World War. This traditional implement shed
was built in the 1920s and Ron can recall as a boy helping his father roof it.
Using straw grown especially for the purpose, the roof was cut and laid in such
a way as to keep out the rain. Even now, more than half a century on, it is still
a highly functional building, with a range of tools and implements
housed within it, quietly waiting to be used.

Ron and Glenda's farm comprises a number of substantial buildings, some using
the distinctive white limestone and orange mortar of the area. The buildings are
a testament to the labour of several generations in the marginal Mallee country.

Rusty

Rusty is a retired drover and grazier. He and his wife retired to a small
town near Tamworth after a lifetime of working on cattle stations.
Rusty spends a lot of his time in his shed, where he makes greenhide
whips for people who appreciate his skills. He still brings out his old
squeezebox now and then, playing the traditional tunes that he and
his friends have performed at country dances since his childhood.
Rusty doesn't have much time for country and western music.
"You can't play guitar on the back of a horse," he says scornfully.
"But the squeezebox you can put into a sugarbag and take anywhere."

Luxmore

Luxmore lives out on a farm with more sheds than he can be bothered counting; some are up gullies he hasn't visited in years. At least a few of them are chock full of the sort of old gear that makes inner-city antique and curio dealers drool. You know the kind of thing — an old soft-drink crate with a few wormholes which, when scrubbed up and varnished, is given an outrageous price tag as genuine Australiana. It doesn't pay to get too clever with Luxmore, though. He may wear those old Police and Fireman braces, but he knows full well that the 1964 Falcon ute with only 30,000 miles on the clock is worth a packet. That's why the locals say he's been known to shoot first and ask questions later if you go driving around his place at night. Be warned, junk dealers.

Rule 1: Never throw anything out

One tradition of the farm shed which still survives in the urban equivalent is hoarding. "You never know when you'll find a use for that" is a common excuse for the elaborate storage of vast supplies of string, timber offcuts, pieces of electrical conduit, nuts and bolts, oddly shaped (but somehow useful-looking) pieces of metal and thousands of other bits and pieces.

The most important thing to remember about stored stuff — and, in fact, about having a shed — is not whether you actually *do* anything with all these fabulous resources; rather, it's the potential of what these things *could* be that's the exciting thing.

And when you finally do find a use for that old clock part you put away 17 years ago or that 10-year-old punctured bicycle tube, the thrill, the satisfaction, is like none other. You have shown admirable foresight, practicality and economy of resources.

Like all great wisdom, there are entirely practical and sensible reasons at the heart of the "never chuck out" tradition. The experience of the Great Depression is often invoked by older shed owners, and such memories of poverty die hard. But they're not the only people annoyed at the flagrant wastefulness of modern living. European migrants who

went through the hardships of the Second World War are also highly conscious of waste. One shed owner tells of a neighbouring Hungarian couple who had kept every paper and plastic shopping bag since 1947. Their hallway was a dark tunnel lined with neatly folded and stacked bags.

There's a bit of a revival going on when it comes to hoarding and storing stuff. This is particularly so when it comes to timber, the prices for which are steadily rising around the world. Consequently there's now a whole new wave of younger shed owners who, like their fathers before them, are accumulating a satisfying collection of offcuts and breadboard-size bits of wood that look far too good to throw out. They're discovering the richness that lies within such frugality.

Keep a thing
for seven years . . .

When Ross (shown here with his son David on the left) moved down to the city from the bush he found he had a lot of stuff to take with him. "When you live in the bush you have to do things yourself," says Ross. "If you do it yourself you'll also know that it's been done properly."

Ross believes that it's important to have enough things on hand to be able to complete a job satisfactorily. "If you keep a thing for seven years, you'll find a use for it," he explains. His shed is an organised space, despite the appearance of vast quantities of apparently random gear.

The Depression and the war years taught Ross the importance of having a comprehensive shed, giving rise to the notion that it is best to buy the tool, not the article.

The return of thrift

Lee is an artist whose shed is an integral part of his work. With a view over
a small, leafy garden, this naturally lit space is true shed rather than
a "studio". Some of Lee's work currently involves weaving baskets and traps
from creepers and vines found in suburban gardens, making useful objects
from stuff that other people would simply dump in the rubbish bin.
In a similar way his shed is made from bits of found timber, iron and
"junk" merged into a pleasing whole.

"My shed grows organically," Lee says. "Come back in four years' time and
it'll be bigger." His shed is a statement about a consumer society in which
people are defined by what they buy instead of what they save.

Lee makes a subsistence living from his artwork and from gardening.
Thrift is on the way back.

Tool heaven

This shed is a memorial to tools. Trevor has amassed an enormous collection of planes, saws, drills and other woodworking tools. "It started out as a hobby but it's gotten out of control," says Trevor. His pride and joy is his plane collection, with instruments ranging from a tiny violin maker's plane to a massive five-foot cooper's plane. Drawer after drawer reveals obscure and curious-looking instruments in steel and wood, often possessing an elegant functionality.

In the tradition of craftsmen passing on their tools from father to son, some of the old wooden planes have had many generations of use. The places where thumbs and fingers have grasped the tool have, over many decades, worn deep depressions in the beech patina. Even so, it's possible to trace the manufacturer's stamps from the early days of the Industrial Revolution. Many of these tools have had a history longer than white Australia's — coming to Australia in an immigrant's luggage, or having been used to make what is now valuable early colonial furniture.

Trevor hopes one day to open up his collection as a museum.
It will be a fine spot to visit.

Small beauties

Bob is one of the hidden talents that reside in Australia's sheds.
A retired toolmaker and production engineer, he makes beautiful,
scaled-down vintage cars in this very shed. Wheel hubs, cowlings, door
panels and all sorts of parts that would normally require a whole car plant
to produce are fabricated by some cleverly made tools, a lathe, ingenuity,
patience and a big store of bits and pieces. ("I'm a bit of a bowerbird,"
confesses Bob.) His cars are even driveable — a small chainsaw motor
means they can chug around the backyard very nicely.

Bob has nothing but disdain for the chequebook restorers, the yuppies
who pester him to sell one of his beautiful miniature Bentleys or Jaguars.
The more they pester him, the less likely he is to sell. What a luxury . . .

The backyard mechanics' institute

Brian's shed is a model of practical self-sufficiency and order.
Even the twine for tying up tomatoes is ranked in order of length.

The shed itself was bought second-hand, unbolted and reassembled
in Brian's backyard. The *pièce de résistance* is the small study —
the back of a pantechnicon which was removed from its chassis and
bolted onto the side of the shed. A firm floor, some old carpet and
electricity then provides the basis for a cosy little study area.

Brian believes in the virtues of self-improvement — a trade union
tradition that harks back to the days of mechanics' institutes and workers'
educational programmes. Not that Brian's shed is all given over to
such earnestness. In one corner, a piece of floral cloth hides a huge,
gleaming Ducati motorbike in immaculate condition.
Several times a month Brian dons his leathers and disappears over
the horizon, blowing out the cobwebs as the bike leans into
yet another corner at high speed . . .

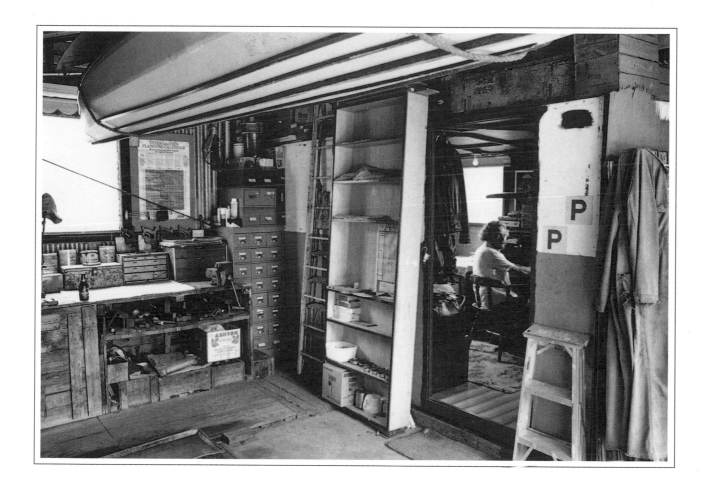

In praise of disorder

Order and disorder in the domestic shed are one of the great sticking points of domestic harmony. In a home that is the very picture of good taste, organised and polished to within an inch of its life, why does the bloke insist on having this revolting festering wound of a shed?

The shed is an outbreak of dirt and chaos in what is otherwise a serenely ordered world. And therein lies the secret. If life has been reduced to a series of routines, there's a powerful need for a safety valve that allows the pressure of organisation, appearances and expectation to be released. The shed is that valve, somewhere to go a bit slack.

Why should everything in the domestic environment be totally ordered? Aren't such attitudes simply the product of reading too many home-decorating magazines? It doesn't have to be that way. As one shed owner said, "Once everything is organised you might as well be dead, because there's nothing else to do."

The creeping demand for total domestic order is, no doubt, based on sound scientific principles for exterminating all vermin and disease, but it means that there are no mysteries for kids to explore, no unplanned areas of unknown around the home in which unimaginable things may lurk. How can

Australian kids ever hope to run the clever country if they have no grasp of shed culture and the great potential that lies within bent pieces of wire and old washers? And does it mean that they'll run screaming from the first sight of a redback spider at age 27?

It's the potential of what can happen in a shed that really matters, not what actually takes place. If it's totally ordered then that potential is less likely to be realised: it's just a shed. Instead, it's far more satisfying for work to be in progress, to have limitless possibilities waiting to happen.

Of course, there's nothing really wrong with an ordered shed. Arranging possessions in a systematic way can give a shed owner a great sense of satisfaction — the joy of meeting the challenge of cataloguing so many diverse bits of stuff. It means that, finally, he can sit back and enjoy the majesty of it all spread before him.

Arguments concerning ordered versus disordered sheds will no doubt continue to be voiced for as long as sheds exist, but ultimately it's not important how your shed looks — as long as you've *got* a shed.

Personal compost

Brian has a great shed. He has collected a wondrous array of treasures and
has arranged them in a witty and enjoyable way.

There's a stuffed dingo with a doll in its mouth, a brass Buddha smoking
a giant pipe, a throne-like chair covered with kangaroo skin.

Here is a person who gains immense satisfaction from his shed,
"turning it over," he says, "like personal compost." Brian is a shining example
of the benefits of accumulation.

The feral shed

If anyone thinks that a good shed is something that only old codgers have, then think again, because David's shed is only four years old. It's a place for swapping bike parts and for creative experimentation of all kinds. Bikes and sheds go hand in hand.

David collects stuff, really good stuff sometimes, from around the street. Some of it is turned into art. He likes old stuff because it's often more robust, enduring and easier to fix than the new, plasticky equivalent. "I like old things because you can use them. I like the way they're made. Old tools are more beautiful. I can't explain it . . ." Take the bicycle he's leaning on. It weighs a ton and has one of those really hard leather seats, but it still works. Will the same be true of a K-Mart mountain bike in 60 years' time?

David lives at the back of his shed in a suite of tiny rooms made out of packing crates.

Everything

Bill lives out of town on a big block of land where he has acres of stuff,
some stored in sheds and some just out in paddocks. Some of the sheds are piled
so high that opening the door reveals an impenetrable wall of things.
There are cardboard boxes full of magazines, car parts, second-hand paint,
kitchen appliances, early computers, video games, cake tins full of springs,
rolls of sandpaper, vinyl toys, barbecuing tools, spark plugs (new and old),
combination screwdrivers, TV products from the 1970s, chemicals,
ironing-board covers and thousands of other things too numerous to name.
This is a treasure trove, where everything is potentially valuable,
where everything has an equal right to existence.

Bill goes to lots of clearance sales, often buying job lots in order to purchase
one particular car part or object of value. He sells some of his stuff, but
the rest is kept waiting for that time when it may become valuable.
"Some boxes I haven't even opened yet," says Bill.

Some people don't like disorder. Bill doesn't seem to mind it.

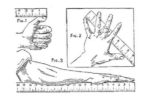

A place where I make the rules

Australian blokes are pretty lucky, there's no doubt about it. Many of them do have a space that they can call their own — their shed. Does it mean that they're simply ducking out of their family responsibilities or are they genuinely alienated within their own homes?

Retirement, for many men, brings a realisation that the domestic space which they have shared for so many years is clearly the domain of the female partner and that it is not easy for the patterns of a lifetime to change. "You put down a cup of coffee on a table in the house," said one shed owner, "and a moment later the wife

swoops down with a dishcloth, lifts the cup up and wipes away a possible coffee ring stain. You get the message soon enough, I'll tell ya."

Social pressures have traditionally assigned women the responsibility for raising a family, a task that requires a degree of control over the whole house. Aware of this fact and the limits it puts on his freedom, a bloke craves a place of his own, a space where he can maintain his identity and maybe even repair it when necessary. Like a shed, for instance. "Somewhere I can put something down and it will still be there next week," says one shed owner.

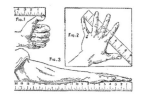

There is a saying uttered by the wives of newly retired men which goes, "I married my husband for better or for worse but not for lunch every day." Spare a thought for the retired man banished to his shed with his lunch box at 8 am, not to return to the house until 5.30 pm.

It would be a mistake to underestimate the importance of sheds in men's lives. Many men clearly do feel a sense of powerlessness with their lot in life, and a small space of their own does not seem too much to ask. It affords them a sense of independence and autonomy while at the same time maintaining the family unit at close hand.

The shed can be a refuge from turbulent times, a constant when all around is changing.

Some men do withdraw to their sheds like a hermit crab into a shell, creating shed widows and shed orphans. Marriages and families have been known to fall apart as a result of men spending too much time in sheds. What we need is a happy medium.

Plenty of women are discovering the joys of shed-type spaces — sewing rooms are a traditional example. Increasing numbers of women are building their own sheds — but that's another book . . .

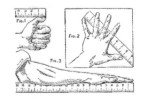

The family therapist

Dr Michael Lee, shown here on the left with his son and father, is a family therapist who takes a professional interest in the role of the shed in Australian family life. He classifies sheds in a range from benign to malignant. A benign shed, like the one shown here, is one which has no capacity to sustain life. In fact, it would probably only contain a few nasty garden chemicals. From there, the scale shifts upwards until it reaches the malignant category: a shed with many life-sustaining properties — fridge, stove, phone, computer, even a bed. Many of the sheds in this book are deeply malignant.

While Michael's analysis is light hearted, he does acknowledge that there is a disturbing side to the divisions within families about spaces and the role of men. Men do retreat to their sheds and it is often difficult to coax them back into the main framework of family life. Some, no doubt, would argue that they're completely happy where they are.

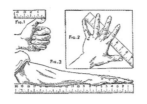

"They're lining up at the barrier for race number 8 at Randwick . . ."

Listening to the races is a time-honoured shed occupation.
Bart does not have a spectacular shed, but it is a good place to listen to the races
under the pretext of doing a job. To make the task easier, there's an old fridge;
all that tension of wondering whether your nag will come home or not
gives the shed punter a dry mouth.

There was once a time when to have a phone line from the shed to
your bookie was the height of covert punting luxury. Now, with
the development of cable TV, satellites, mobile phones, computers and the whole
information highway, the shed punter could soon become a thing of the past.

Listening to the cricket remains an ideal shed activity, however.
Even one-day cricket is sufficiently leisurely and affable to make pleasant
shed radio. Over many years, ABC cricket commentators have polished
their art to create a hazy, matey atmosphere where time does not matter and
the sleepy pace is only occasionally broken by a flurry of high-pitched
comments culminating in, "He's out!"

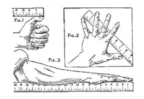

Small is beautiful

Murray's shed is proof that you don't need a large space to have
a successful and satisfying shed. He has lived in his inner-city house most of
his life and in the corner of his small backyard is a shed of about 2 square metres.
"Everything I need to fix anything around the house is in here," Murray
proudly says of his compact little shed. Hidden deftly in nooks and crannies are
car repair tools, serious plumbing implements and shoe repair materials.
There's even space for a small seat, under which is a useful supply of home brew.

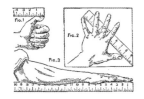

Shed philosopher

It's a little hard to put your finger on exactly what it is that Jeffrey
does in his shed. He listens to the radio, smokes his pipe, has
a home-brew beer occasionally (a good drop, too) and, in his own words,
"renovates cardboard boxes." In short, he revels in his shed,
pondering its qualities and generally considering life.
That's fine, Jeffrey. That's what sheds are for.

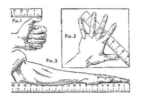

The male end

Graham and his family live out in the bush in a sort of semicircle of buildings that were once "temporary" but have now become permanent. On the far tip of one side of this semicircle is Graham's shed.

Towards the middle of the semicircle are the kids' rooms and the kitchen and family area. On the far side of the arc is his partner Vicki's sewing workroom, full of doilies, lace, dresses and Victorian ladies' gewgaws. It's a spectrum which embraces both a masculine and feminine sense of order, and is a clever solution to the usual problem of the "ownership" of domestic space.

And there's nothing significant about the swastika stencilled on the dressmaker's dummy.

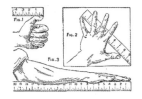

The best home workshop in the state, without a doubt

Geoff's a Ford man. He has dozens of car manuals and a vast tool collection
for working on his beloved Fords. A successful retired garage proprietor,
he spends long hours in his workshop, fine-tuning his panel van
to enable it to reach very high speeds.

Not only does his shed have a specially strengthened floor, there's a luxury
for the home workshop: a hoist. It's a pretty neat shed, too. Geoff says
he signed a contract with his wife to keep it clean.

Geoff's shed has a claim to fame: it was officially opened by Joh Bjelke-
Petersen, the then Premier of Queensland, in a shed-launching party.
There's even a small plaque, unveiled at the time, proclaiming this fact.

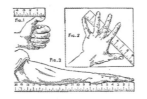

When you get married, buy a shed

These two men have lived across the road from each other since childhood and have been hanging out in Graeme's shed (that's Graeme on the right and Steve on the left) ever since.

His shed, Graeme says, is "nothing special", but it has all the basics required for a classic shed: the beer fridge covered in stickers, framed posters of FJ Holdens, a fine collection of blues CDs and tapes, a mighty solid workbench (fished out of a nearby river), a potbelly stove to make it habitable during the winter, and even — a rarity these days — a calendar featuring a topless woman.

Graeme is slowly fixing up a 1948 BSA Bantam. His advice for young blokes when they get married is "buy a shed — you need a space to call your own."

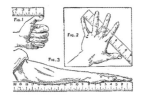

The tragedy of the shedless

Eric lives in a rented house, and he's a shed orphan. Landlords take
a dim view of tenants setting up sheds. They probably worry that
one day they may have to clean them up.

Lamenting the plight of the tenant, Eric says, "A rented shed is never
quite yours. You can't get settled down." Layers of personal history are not
allowed to accumulate in a rented shed. There's no chance of developing
a rich stew of objects and projects, safe in the knowledge that they can
rest undisturbed for years on end if necessary.

What does this un-met yearning do for the shedless? They hang around
the sheds of others or just shut that part of their lives off completely.
The flat dweller, the urbanly consolidated, the tenant, have all had to
anaesthetise the urge to have a good shed. There's probably a whole
new range of therapy opportunities opening up . . .

The social shed

It would be a mistake to assume that the suburbs of Australia are populated with glum men sitting idly in their sheds tinkering with tools and bits of wood.

There are plenty of sheds out there that are virtually the centre of family life. For instance, it is the tradition in some Australian-Mediterranean families that many of the messier jobs of family life take place not in the main house but in the shed. The killing of livestock clearly cannot happen in the sparklingly clean kitchen. The same goes for cooking large meals for family events — it's better to let the smell stink out the shed rather than have it permeate the house. Canning and preserving the products of the home garden is another example. Likewise, the making and sharing of home-brew beer is now a massive shed pastime. All these activities help to reinforce family links and traditions, in addition to being good fun.

In Australian culture there is also the purpose-built party shed, an example of which, sadly, was not found for this book. The distinguishing feature of this possibly mythological shed is the bare concrete floor, which slopes down to a central drainage point. This facilitates cleaning up on the morning after the party:

a hose is brought in and all spilt beer, cigarette ash, vomit and assorted party by-products are flushed away, allowing the shed to return to more mundane purposes.

Specialised beer-cooling facilities are another feature of the party shed. These facilities could be anything from a row of partially broken-down domestic fridges or special cooling troughs. Barbecues are generally associated with such sheds, especially the massive purpose-built type that can accommodate 300 sausages and 150 chops at the same time. A row of coloured lights along the rafters can often be a sign that what appears to be a normal shed is, in fact, a closet party shed.

However, these are the exception. Social sheds can be of the most benign kind, such as the family rumpus room.

By lining the walls with plywood and improving the floor surface, a functional and reasonably clean place can be created that's ideally suited to storing teenagers for long periods of time.

Like so many of our concepts about sheds, the rumpus room derives heavily from American cultural influences of the 1950s. How many of the baby-boomer generation recall all those *Popular Mechanics* magazines, showing a genial pipe-smoking Dad in a check flannel shirt labouring away on a project while a couple of freckle-faced kids watched on in admiration? The impact of those influences is still being felt in sheds around the country as those former freckle-faced children attempt to recreate the myth of the Handy Dad.

The party shed

Dave and his wife Carole have converted his garage into
a party shed/bar known as the Trade Union Tavern. It's a pub in
their own backyard, featuring decorations from around the world.
Ned Kelly stands behind the bar, his arms folded defiantly.
Photos decorate the walls in proof of the many parties that have
taken place here. There's also a Lenin corner — John Lennon on
one side, Vladimir Illych Lenin on the other.

Party sheds take many forms.

The rumpus room

This is Simon's family rumpus room. It was once a shed but has now
been lined, carpeted and decorated with sundry Americana.
This sort of conversion was a sizeable building job, yet it didn't require
the local council's permission, nor a degree in engineering.
It's a perfect demonstration of domestic male capability.

Rumpus rooms were the sorts of things you read about in *Popular Mechanics*
magazines in the 1950s and '60s. A slightly more legitimate sort of space
than your classic shed, the rumpus room still offers the opportunity for
the sort of experimentation and exploration not possible in the main house.

Simon is pleased with the fact that the kids can muck around here safely
and that parties can be held without too much concern for cleanliness.
He would possibly allow limited indoor footy in this rumpus room.

Inner-city farmhouse

Francesco's shed is a kind of farmhouse, even though he lives in an inner-city suburb. It's here he keeps the tools for his highly productive garden, preserves and makes sauces from vegetables, and stores the chook food. There's also a stove that may prove useful for cooking up big meals which would otherwise fill the main house — proudly scrubbed clean and bright as a button — with smells.

The shed is the place where, back in the old country, the significant seasonal events took place. For this reason it's an important part of the family's cultural life.

Backyard bakers

Ross's shed is part of another intensively cultivated inner-suburban backyard. The main focus is the traditional domed Calabrian oven, which produces crusty wood-oven bread.

Every Saturday morning before dawn, Ross and his brothers go down to their father's backyard and fire up the oven, burning packing-crate timber and eucalypt wood to heat the brick. Meanwhile they mix the flour, water and yeast in another shed. As the dough rises they check the temperature of the oven by cooking slivers of dough and testing its internal consistency. When the tub of dough has risen and the oven is judged close to ready, they slice the dough with the casual efficiency of a job learned by time and tradition. The oven is swept clean of ash, the loaves slid in on long-handled wooden shovels and the door closed.

As the bread bakes, its massive rich smell billows over the neighbours' yards. Finally, Ross and his brothers sample some home-grown wine and enjoy homemade salami and marinated fennel accompanied by fresh hot bread dipped in olive oil . . .

Shedoscope

For many years, John had a 15-seat cinema in his shed.
Back in the early 1960s it was relatively cheap and easy to get
8 mm sound feature versions of recently released films. So John's
friends and neighbours would gather on a Saturday night to watch the
latest John Wayne epic or Gidget movie. There were curtains on the walls,
dimable lights, a bio box — in fact, the full cinematic experience in
the back shed. Unfortunately, the rise and rise of the video has meant
that the back-shed movie theatre is no longer viable, and John's
cinema has fallen into disuse.

A shed gives you hope

Geoff's shed is, in his own words, a world of its own.
A former Telecom employee, Geoff is an expert at restoring old phones,
especially those from the earlier part of this century. His shed is a busy spot
because it is very much a social centre for other old telephone specialists
who gather to barter, swap and generally natter about old phones and parts.
With a potbelly stove for winter warmth, the dog for company and, of course,
a telephone, it's a fairly sophisticated and comfortable shed.

Geoff clearly derives great benefit from his hideaway. "You can't get out
of physiotherapy what you get out of your shed," he says.

Bert's boxing shed

Bert and his boxing shed are an institution in his neighbourhood.
They've both been there for about 30 years. Bert built the shed
in his backyard not long after he came out from Ireland. Even now
his accent is so thick that one has to listen carefully to his tales of
promising youngsters who have come and gone, some gone on
to better things, some gone bad.

After nearly 20 years he still works as a bouncer in the local pub.
With surprising speed and force he can give a quick demo of how to
turn around a troublesome customer. He's still a hard man.

Skipping or doing speedball work among deformed punching
bags, the local youngsters pay close attention to his instructions.
This is a serious shed. No fooling around here.

The garage band

No collection of shed photos would be complete without the obligatory garage band. "Garage band" has become synonymous with harsh and noisy music — which is how most music tends to sound in an empty tin shed.

Here are Cane and his mates, thrashing out their own versions of rock/grunge/funk in Mum's garage. It's a place of noise and fun, of youthful dreaming of fame and fortune. The neighbours hate it.

Dedicated garage band enthusiasts get serious and start collecting old mattresses, egg cartons and ancient curtains in order to line the walls to produce that perfect, low-budget acoustic environment. Once that happens, they'll never be out of there.

The shed economy

Thousands of Australian businesses have started in the back shed. From humble origins, massive businesses have grown into vast factories and corporate empires spanning the globe.

On the other hand, thousands of businesses have also been quite happy to stay in the shed, tinkering around and making enough to get by. These are our true shed heroes: decent people who aren't out to make the big quid but will generally do a pretty good job at a fair price.

Without a massive corporate infrastructure to support, such people can ease themselves out of business towards the end of their working lives while still dabbling as the whim takes them. None of that shock-of-retirement nonsense for them.

It's also possible for them to conduct their business at a leisurely pace. If a mate drops around, you can generally find the time to share a beer or a cup of coffee. You can always come back later to finish the job you left off.

A sense of capability is very important to many of these shed owners. Having the ability to make something useful, valued, well made and functional is a boost to the shed owner's self-esteem.

Many retired captains of industry (especially engineers) have fantastic sheds. They have the resources and the skills to get together sheds that are the equivalent of small

factories. Lathes, pipe benders, drill presses, saws and dozens of other pieces of large machinery can be found in many of these well-equipped sheds. Their owners are often secretive about what they contain, partly because the contents are so valuable.

What is also surprising is how many of these shed owners know of the existence of each other's sheds. There's a whole network of specialist shed people out there: during the writing of this book, many shed owners recognised each other or suggested the names of others who had sheds worth looking at. "Ted's your man to see about old lawn-mower parts," or, "If it's bending glass you want, speak to Kevin. Here's his number."

Even more interesting is the semi-cashless nature of this hidden sector of the economy. Beer currency is common (that is, one slab for a bit of welding), or just a notional exchange of built-up favours that can be called upon at some future date when they may be necessary.

For the sake of avoiding undesirable scrutiny from the taxation authorities it may be better to say no more . . .

The serious backyard workshop

George's shed is more of a small backyard factory than a shed.
A retired engineer, George has bought up old government machinery
whenever it's become obsolescent, or the contents of old workshops when
they've closed down. Consequently he has at his disposal the same capability
to bend, shape and cut metal as a small metalworking factory.

It's a large shed that has grown from a two-car garage to a space
three times that size, encompassing and enclosing a tree and having
distinct sections for different activities.

There's a sense of relentless activity about the place; such massive and
ordered productivity must have required a great deal of energy and drive.
Any large Australian city would have hundreds of people like George
labouring away in their backyard workshops.

In case you were wondering, that's an Ariel Square 4 in the foreground.

Just about anything

Rob is a resourceful man. Here, in the smaller of his two sheds,
he restores motorbikes, makes moulds, casts metal parts and even makes
his own nuts and bolts. A wide range of metalworking machinery gives his little
home workshop the capacity to make authentic parts for motorcycles and model
steam trains. The quality and detail of the finished job is extraordinary:
tiny oil pumps, secured by minute handmade bolts, pump oil through
copper pipes half the thickness of a matchstick. Rob is basically self-taught —
he just likes making things at home.

While he can cast a wide range of hard-to-get motorcycle and car parts,
he doesn't want to turn it into a production line. "It's just a hobby," says Rob.
"I mainly make things for mates."

"I wouldn't pay anybody to do anything I can do myself"

Bob is a busy man (a government minister at the time of this photograph)
and values the break from work that his garage-cum-shed affords him.
As a former metalworker he's very proud of his manual skills.
"I wouldn't pay anybody to do anything I can do myself," he says,
displaying some of the tools he has made in the past.

Bob's workshop is not the standard corrugated iron shed but the understorey
of his home. This is a common form of shed in some parts of Australia.

Fertility and hard work

Napoleon's shed is too small and dark inside to photograph.
It contains gardening tools and rows of preserves, olives and olive oil.
Made from flattened oil drums and second-hand corrugated iron and
featuring large, overhanging eaves that create a shaded outside work space,
the shed is an important part of Napoleon's small and highly productive
backyard farm. Many years diligent work have turned the poor soil of
his family's original building block into a fertile little market garden.

Instruments for creation

David's main source of income is to sell old tools through a market stall. Sheds are the places where his potential stock lies, elusive antique tools perhaps 200 years old waiting to be discovered. "They're instruments for creation," says David, "and they usually come with interesting people full of great stories to tell. My stall attracts these sort of blokes. It's a sort of exchange point for memories."

David uses his own shed as a place to clean up old tools before their sale. The trick is to remove as much of the rust and gunge as possible but to make sure that both the metal and wood have the patina that comes from years of use and contact with the hand.

The shed professional

Les works for a shed manufacturer that goes by the reassuring name of "Galeprufe". As such, he's in an excellent position to tell us in which direction the Australian shed is going. Les says that as steel is now cheaper than timber, most sheds today are all steel construction instead of part timber, part steel. Sheds are, on average, also getting bigger, with a greater demand for sheds up to 30' x 20' x 8'.

According to Les, the shed is increasingly being seen as part of the family's living arrangements. Due to ever-tighter planning restrictions there is a growth in heritage sheds — the mock neo-federation shed, complete with finials and similar decorations designed to blend in with the neighbourhood. Shed purists may consider such attempts to disguise the classic galvanised simplicity of the shed a travesty and an insult.

Fathers and sons (and daughters too)

Is there a secret knowledge that men hand on to their sons in sheds? What values are handed on by older men to young men in the seclusion of the shed? Is there a case for saying that the shed is the equivalent of the Navajo smokehouse or the Papuan Longhaus, to which only men are admitted?

Surely there's a massive amount of anthropological work yet to be done on this curly subject. Then again, maybe it's better left alone; we blokes don't want that sort of interference.

During the compilation of this book, a number of men

pointed out that if you wanted to have some sort of chat with your father, you had to go out to the shed. Conversation tends to be a by-product of the endeavour at hand, be it straightening nails extracted from old timber or holding onto something while Dad works on it. Working on cars is a classic example of an occasion where things are learnt by experience and observation. Once it was almost considered automatic that sons learnt "handy" skills from their fathers in this way. Nowadays there are different kinds of domestics spaces (flats and smaller houses) and

infinitely more glamorous rivals for the attentions of young men: television, video games and different social options. The shed simply cannot compete.

Most blokes need a reason or an excuse to enjoy one another's company. It's not a comfortable subject for them to discuss. Many men seemed a little hesitant to talk about the pleasure of spending time with their fathers or sons, unless they were reminiscing about the past.

Perhaps the secret message that has to be said nowadays is, "Look son, it's all right to be handy about the house, there's no shame in it. You can work on being sensitive at some other time . . ."

The early-matured shed

Paul is reasonably proud of his shed because, while it's not all that old, it has managed to acquire an air of being a mature site of worthy accumulated stuff — like good cheese. Notice, for instance, the large collection of timber offcuts beside Paul's head. This is a man who has clearly embraced the shed principle that you should never throw anything out if you think it might be useful.

His son Rogan spends some time in the shed with him, but it's hard to tell whether any secret father-to-son knowledge has passed between them.

Paul has 11 ladders. He didn't say anything about it; a friend of his, easily impressed by such information, came up with this fact. Modesty concerning one's shed is definitely a good thing.

Learning by osmosis

Three generations (from left: Matthew, Allan and John) are shown here
sharing a shed. "I can make a mess in the shed and it's all right because
I make the rules," says Allan. It's been a highly productive mess over the years,
with cupboards, chairs, a boat and bassinets all finding their way here.
John observes that whatever he learnt about woodworking and repairing
he gained by osmosis rather than through direct instruction.
This is very much the preferred way for generations to hand on
secret male-to-male knowledge.

A dream that one day . . .

Terry says that sheds are a space to dream in — a place of limitless possibilities waiting to happen. Even though his own shed tends to get used for drying washing and as a sorting area, he still intends to get around to make something of it. "You see a lot of half-finished projects in sheds," says Terry.

And yes, that's a Stanley knife that his son is proudly holding in his hand.

Dick's daughters

Dick's shed is a place of memory. At his funeral, one of his daughters sprinkled over his coffin shavings gathered from the floor of his shed instead of the traditional rose petals. Now, more than a year after his death, the shed provides a link to his memory for his daughters and sons-in-law. Talking of her father, one daughter draws in the air the outline of the old man standing at his bench, invoking a startlingly imaginable figure. Another picks up an odd little cup made from a cut-down jam tin and muses over its practical economy. Dick was a man far ahead of his time in recycling and other sound environmental habits.

It's a wonderful shed. A lifetime's collection of skills and knowledge have been condensed into a practical order that is at once systematic yet agreeably casual: tools clustered together on a rack made with a few artful twists of wire; latches, handles and hinges made from carefully cut and soldered metal and wire. There's no waste here.

For the family, the shed poses a quandary: what should happen to this space? Should it be preserved as a common family area (great for the sons-in-law to come down and use the power tools), or will its contents start to rust from lack of care and attention now that the shed's busy days are over? The answer seems clear. The pull of the shed is strong, and having survived this long, it will probably see a few more serviceable years yet.

Retiring to the bench

Australian men retire to their sheds and then they die. This elephant's graveyard view of the Australian shed should be tempered with another view: without a shed to go to, Australian men would probably die even more quickly.

Many retired men feel that their shed is a lifeline. Behind the sniggers and the jokes from some quarters it is obvious that there is a genuine need for men to have a meditative space that allows for both creative expression and purposeful activity.

In the sheds of retired men around Australia there is also an extraordinary amount of accumulated skill and talent not being put to use. Such is the distrust and uncertainty between the generations, however, that there is unlikely to be a spontaneous outbreak of cranky old metalworkers giving wayward youths useful tips on fixing up their clapped-out Holdens or demonstrating the glory of the ancient art of brazing.

A number of the older shed owners interviewed during the research for this book *did* mention that they would quite like to pass on their skills, but mostly they were too shy to do so. This is a sorry situation, but perhaps sorrier still is the state of shedlessness which afflicts many elderly men. Shedlessness is most evident when older couples move into a retirement village: a rich shed, an accumulation of up to 60 years of shed activity, must be culled down to a few small handtools or, worse still, nothing at all. Those retirement homes that don't allow men a little space to muck around in are especially tragic. Space is already at a premium in such places. No wonder some of their inhabitants often feel that a useful life is over.

Retirement can be a stressful business. Some men positively look forward to the shed in their retirement; they view it as a focus for creative activities denied them in their working lives. One man spoke of a neighbour, a former police officer, who the day after his retirement went out and bought a substantial wood lathe because he'd always dreamed of the unique satisfaction of revealing the beauty of timber on a humming lathe.

For some men, retirement brings a realisation that despite a lengthy working life as a breadwinner, they have few friends and that the friends they had at work were only acquaintances with whom they shared the hours 9 'til 5. Some men contrast the way in which women seem to establish better friendships with other women. These are troubling matters for all men to consider, but perhaps particularly so for the retired man.

Ted

This is a shed which has truly seen a lifetime of experience. Ted, its owner,
a former electrician at Holden's, retired some time in the 1950s. Since then
he has put his shed to good use. It has a comprehensive range of equipment for
the home workshop, with plenty of well-made storage drawers (those old Singer
treadle sewing machine drawers have found many a happy home in a shed).

On the bench is a small homemade steam engine in the process of being
soldered together from old cans and pipes as a gift for a distant great-grandchild.
Toys that demonstrated the basic principles of physics such as this were once
quite common but have since been replaced by SegaMegadrives and suchlike.
It's nice to know that someone's still making the stuff that makes you think.

Busier than ever

Down the end of this shed, creepers have started to strangle some old kids' bicycles. But in the middle, newly varnished croquet mallets hang from the roof. Even though he's retired, ex-woodwork teacher Alan still passes on his valuable skills. Several times a week he teaches young women the basics of woodworking. He shows off their work with an offhand dismissiveness that does not conceal a certain pride in their achievements under his tutelage.

Like so many men who find that their skills are still sought even in retirement, Alan wonders how he ever had time to work. Nevertheless, he appreciates the fact that now he can choose to do things when he feels like it.

A local institution

Josef has retired with his wife to a small seaside town, where he has established a substantial shed in the backyard. It's very important to him. "I'd be lost without it," he says. "You might as well put me in a pine box as separate me from my shed."

Although Josef's shed is connected to the main house by an intercom, it has many useful domestic features, including various cooking arrangements (great for barbecuing local seafood) and an enormous cool room with a very substantial supply of home-brew beer.

Clearly, Josef has a well-set-up shed. The locals speak of it with admiration.

A place to relax

Joe has a compact shed in which he enjoys a daily afternoon nap.
It's a very organised little space with all manner of tools tucked away
behind curtains. There's even an old treadle sewing machine ideal for
stitching canvas, a by-product of spending some of his life working as a rigger.
Joe is well known in his neighbourhood as a handy person when
it comes to repairing things made of canvas and rope.

Don's multi-function workshop

Don is a retired cabinet maker. His shed, which is in fact a series of
rooms dedicated to various hobbies such as wood turning and gem cutting,
is a well-ordered space. This is often the case with retired craftsmen,
who regard an orderly work space as a matter of professional pride.
Don still makes beautifully finished wooden objects, such as the fishing
floats by his right hand. His tools are kept in immaculate condition.

There's another reason why Don's shed is important to him:
his young family lived in it while the main house was being built.
It then became a billiards room for his family as they grew up.
Now it's a workshop for Don in his retirement.

Solutions for retirement villages

Retirement homes present quite a problem for some men. The act of moving from a normal suburban house with space for a shed is fraught with problems: frequently the shed and its contents are disposed of in order to fit into a small unit. Retirement homes have been slow to recognise the sense of loss that some men experience when this happens. However, Herb and Dean (left and right) and some of their retirement village friends have avoided this problem by using a double garage as a workshop for their shared use. It has become a major focus of activity and is even seen by the village owners as a marketing advantage.

Herb, Dean and their friends share tools (a delicate matter) and skills, and it's an enjoyable form of socialising for them. "We don't have to worry about time in here," says Herb.

The men joke about how their shed is a bit of a glorified kennel.

The illicit shed

Some sheds never made it to this book. This is because their owners were conscious that their shed activities were not likely to bring approval from various authorities, be they the police or the politically correct.

Top of the list are the home-brewed firewater makers. It seems that nearly every culture has a tradition of making grappa, slivovitz, shed vodka, scrumpy, cherry wine, whatever — as long as it's as near to pure alcohol as possible. Aware of the illegality of their activities, Australian distillers of these fiery liquors go to extraordinary lengths to conceal their distilling apparatus and the operations of their sheds.

One elderly gentleman, who had spent some time in a POW camp after the war, had mastered the art of quickly disassembling his still and scattering its components around the shed so as to seem part of the general shed paraphernalia.

Growing marijuana under lights is another highly illicit shed activity. This involves large quantities of electricity, complex switches and watering systems and a very high level of paranoia. One shed dope grower even had an extraction fan with an extremely high chimney to diffuse the resinous smell of his activities.

Pornography and sheds seem to be strongly connected in many people's minds. A number of those interviewed

could recall going to someone's shed at some time in their youth for a buck's night and watching blue movies. Videos may have killed this tradition. The shed with pin-ups of nude women seemed fairly uncommon.

Another type of shed that was not willing to be exposed was the war gamer's shed. At least one militaria fan has a shed filled with full-size trenches, barbed wire, dried mud and duckboards. The idea is to get dressed up in First World War uniforms, grab some beers and sit in a dugout for the afternoon with your mates, listening to 78s on a wind-up record player and getting drunk. The players involved in these activities didn't want to be photographed, as they said people wouldn't understand.

Men like the illegitimacy of the shed. It's not quite acceptable; a shed is for outcasts. If there's anything that's been pinched or is a bit dodgy, it's probably in the shed.

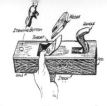

Handy tips for the would-be shed owner

Good basic tools

With the growth in recent years of do-it-yourself culture, many people have gone out and bought themselves tools, often without any understanding of what they should be looking for or what they should be avoiding.

It's unfortunate that there are a great number of very poor quality handtools on the market. As a general rule, cheap tools are to be avoided; they are usually made from poor quality metal and are of such shoddy construction that they will prove your apparently modest investment to be a complete waste of money. There are still good quality tools for sale, generally in specialised hardware and tool shops. They're often expensive, but if looked after will provide many years of good service.

Another option is to buy tools at garage sales, where many a tradesman's tools have gone for a song. It's also true that there are collectors and dealers out there who know exactly how much such tools are worth, so be forewarned.

What to look for

Planes

The bases of most planes aren't 100 per cent level, so it's useful to take a good engineer's rule or steel straightedge with you when you're looking for a second-hand plane.

To check that a plane is not warped or bowed, retract the blade or cutter and lay the straightedge along the base of the plane. There should only be a hair's width of light showing between the plane and the straightedge.

The plane should be clean and in good condition. The cutter is most important; check to see that the back of the blade is not pitted with rust. If it is, it will be impossible to get a sharp edge across the complete width of the blade. Brands and makes to look out for include early Stanley, Record, and the red and black Pope Falcon. Most older American-made planes are pretty good. Steer clear of Chinese-made or Carter planes.

Chisels

Quality brands of chisels to look out for include E.A. Berg (with a blue shark on the handle), Ward, Stanley, Titan and older Marples. There are also a number of very good Swiss brands of chisels. Again, it's important to check that the back is not pitted, otherwise it will be difficult to make a sharp edge.

Saws

Don't buy a bent or kinked saw. It's almost impossible to straighten and will be practically useless. Old saws can be sharpened by a professional saw sharpener (look in the phone book for one near you), bringing impressive improvements for only about $8 to $10.

Good older brands include Philadelphia Diston, Spear and Jackson, Pax, Simonds, Sandersons and Sandvik. As a rough rule of thumb, if it has five holding screws in the handle and is marked London Spring on the blade, it should be very good.

Again, saws of more recent manufacture, even from some of the reputable brands mentioned above, are not necessarily good, so take care in choosing a new saw.

Hammers

A good claw hammer is a must. Don't buy one that has a chipped face — it could deflect dangerously.

The feel of a hammer is probably the most important thing to take into consideration when buying one, as there are not many working parts to go wrong. Bear in mind that a hammer shouldn't be too heavy or too light for the task you have in mind. In theory, the handle of a balanced hammer resting on its claw should be absolutely horizontal. Good brands of hammers include Cheney, Stanley and Cyclone.

Squares

The best way to check whether a square is still right-angled is to place it on a solid surface with a straight edge (such as a piece of chipboard), rule a line along the edge, turn it over and rule another just parallel to it. If the two lines are not parallel, the rule is not absolutely 90 degrees. Whether purchasing a new or old square, be very wary of instruments with wooden handles, as they can warp or twist. Good brands to look out for include Rabone, Starrett and Moore & Wright.

Cleaning and looking after old tools

If you're a vigilant searcher you'll often find very good old tools, despite being covered in rust or grease. There are a number of ways of cleaning such tools. One technique is to soak them in molasses for a period of between two days and two weeks. This should remove most rust. However, all wooden and die-cast parts should be removed from the tool before being soaked in molasses. Molasses is available from stock and feed suppliers.

It is best to experiment with this technique on something that's not of value before trying it on your tool. Some people prefer cleaning with steel-wool and methylated spirits.

Once your tool has been cleaned of rust, paint and other impurities, metal parts should be coated in CRC Longlife or a similar product.

Unless you're using the tool frequently, don't hang it up on the traditional workshop shadow board: it will end up rusting again. Instead, put it away in a dry place such as a drawer or a toolbox, preferably with a film of CRC Longlife over the tool.

If you are interested in information about or identification of older and unusual tools contact:

The Handtool Preservation Association of Australia
PO Box 1163
Carlton Victoria 3053
or

T.J. Rowe
PO Box 49
Myponga South Australia 5202.

Storage

If one is going to accumulate stuff then a bit of storage space may be needed, although just how to store things is the subject of debate among shed owners. Some people prefer random storage, which involves leaving things where they were last put down. The pile theorists (as they're called) say this is good exercise for the brain, as it improves the memory. On the other hand there are those people who prefer to bring a little more organisation to their sheds. They like to store things on shelves and in cupboards.

Whichever system you prefer, you're probably going to need some sort of shelving. You can go down to the local hardware and buy the basic bolt-together zinc-plated steel shelving, but it's a bit uninteresting — and, some would say, overpriced. An alternative is to approach your local fruit and veg shop and ask them if they've got any old wooden boxes they don't need. Stacked one on top of another, these boxes can usually reach a respectable height before they topple over. Some of them still have nice pictures of fruit on the side.

The other option is to go to a house demolition sale. These are usually advertised in the building materials section of the classified ads. If you turn up at the right time you can often pick up some very cheap shelving and adapt it to your purposes. Many of the building demolition yards (found in the Yellow Pages under Building Materials — Second-hand) have good industrial shelving going cheap.

Shed furniture

Never ever buy a new piece of furniture for the shed. A good shed chair is one that would have been thrown out if you hadn't interceded and saved it, even if it's not quite as flash as it once was. It should be strong enough to stand on, so it may need a few extra cross braces — and while you're at it, put an extra cushion on it for comfort.

A dartboard is a vital piece of shed furniture. So too is a picture of Queen Elizabeth II. It doesn't need to indicate any royalist tendencies; rather, it's a sign that the shed is a reservoir of memories and old associations.

Most essential of all is a stable, solid workbench. It needs to be strong enough to withstand something being belted onto its surface with a large hammer. A good test of stability is to jump up and down on top of it; if the bench doesn't move, it's acceptable. Some people prefer traditional wooden workbenches, but the welded steel variety is just as good and likely to be cheaper. Secondhand workbenches are found at garage sales, in junkyards or at auctions.

Now you've got a bench, you'll need a vice to go on it as well. Metal vices are all the go these days — wood vices are relatively rare and are more expensive.

The beer fridge

Sheds get hot in summer, so a beer fridge is a must. The best kind is the large, rounded type, preferably with a lot of chrome. It's often a bit noisy, but at least this tells you the electricity's still on. You might have to keep the door shut with an octopus strap. Then put lots of stickers on it.

Shed radio

The shed radio is one that has been superseded in the house by the all-new CD-playing AM/FM black plastic box.

Inevitably, the shed radio is AM only, and thus is only good for listening to the races or the ranting and raving of talkback pocket-despots.

There are even those serious radio listeners who have had a phone installed in the shed in order to respond to some outrage on the air ("I was just so furious when I heard that young fellow that I had to ring up to say . . .").

Ideally, a good shed radio should have a warm, fuzzy tone, with the speaker hidden behind some of that strange flecked cloth that only ever appeared on 1940s and '50s radios and on your old aunt's large scratchy furniture.

The radio should be of durable construction — something able to withstand a lump of timber powerfully directed towards it — and be missing at least one vital knob. If it has to be switched on and off with a pair of pliers, so much the better.

A television is a rare thing in a shed — unless it's a shed of the totally malignant variety. This is because it's pretty difficult to do something useful and watch TV at the same time. The spirit of the Australian shed poses one of the greatest threats to the universal dominance of television over the minds of the populace.

The true music lover

The genuine connoisseur of good music does not depend on his shed radio as a source of the quality product. He brings his own.

Hence it's possible to find many a shed with a fine collection of greasy but dearly loved tapes ("I always listen to Elmore James when I'm working on a gearbox"). Country and western and blues both fall into the category of favoured shed music, possibly because both are often a little too gritty or maudlin — or worse still, old fashioned — for main-house domestic tastes.

The true shed fan, of course, listens to his music on an 8-track cartridge player. This has the unfortunate problem of restricting the listening range to the three or so years at the end of the 1960s — a period heavily dominated by Perry Como. This shortcoming is, however, compensated for by the pleasure of wiring up a car audio system out of its native environment.

Where do you get a shed from anyway?

This is the easy part. Sheds are big business, and the competition to sell you a shed is cutthroat.

A distinction needs to be drawn between tool sheds and garages. A tool shed is generally a small, flimsy production designed to hold gardening tools and to be less than the minimum size required for council approval.

A garage, on the other hand, is big enough to more than swing a cat, especially if you don't put the car in it. A garage is an ideal basis for a shed.

Shop around for a shed that suits your needs. You can buy garages or tool sheds in kit form or even get them built by tradesmen on your behalf. However, keeping in the spirit of the thing, it's more interesting to explore wider possibilities.

Second-hand sheds

Many older garages are simply made from steel and timber frames bolted together and covered in galvanised iron. It's possible to buy a garage of this kind very cheaply at a demolition sale. All you have to do is pour a slab of cement for the floor, dismantle the structure and reassemble it in your own backyard. That way your new shed will be well on the way to acquiring its veneer of shed credibility — even if it's someone else's.

Other built structures

The bodies of old vans, pantechnicons and other trucks make a fine basis for a shed. Again, they already have that friendly, used look about them. Never mind that they get hot as Hades in the summer.

You could always make a shed yourself from old sheets of metal and backyard junk. You may need a few essential framing pieces from the many handyman iron and steel shops that sell iron sections, purlins, frames and so forth (check farming magazines and newspapers for details on these).

You can improvise. Reuse the old iron from the garden fence if the metal is not too far gone. If you make your shed just under the minimum size for council approval, use your imagination to expand it.

With the unending gentrification of most Australian suburbs, some local councils have become design fascists, tightly regulating the appearance of local sheds to fit their notions of order and civic pride. Would you be able to get away with old hammered-out oil tins for a wall? Not if the local council hears about it. It's always best to make a few tentative inquiries first. If you're planning an extensive range of enjoyable activities in your shed, it's advisable to keep your drawings to a bare minimum. Councils get a little concerned when they see lined walls, extensive power points and so on.

The author's shed

Mark has seen a lot of sheds. When he came across this one a few years ago, he knew just how to fit it out. He's pretty pleased with the result; his only complaint is that it's too small.

Working from home with a computer, Mark likes to go to his shed every day for a break. It doesn't matter what he does there — whack a piece of wood, rearrange things or generally muck around — the thing is that he's doing something with his hands.

Mark looks forward to his shed mellowing over the years.

Also by Mark Thomson

STORIES FROM THE SHED

What goes on between blokes and sheds? In *Stories from the Shed*, enthusiasts from around the country come clean and tell it how it really is in the last bastion of Aussie maledom. And apparently it's not all hammers, nails and timber offcuts. Sex, drugs, rock'n'roll, birth and death, great discoveries and tragicomedy to rival Shakespeare—it's all going on in the backyard shed.

Set against a back drop of wall-to-wall stuff, junk, gear, supplies and stock, these funny and affectionate stories, collected by the author of *Blokes & Sheds*, capture the past, present and future of Aussie shedland.

Angus & Robertson
ISBN 0 207 19070 4